HOORAY!

WE HAVE FOUND OUR HERO!

ALSO BY BARBARA FLEMING

The Fishermen of Jesus
Diadem Books, 2010
ISBN 978-1-907294-730

Three Men in a Book
Heroes of the Bible
Diadem Books, 2010
ISBN 978-1-908026-08-8

Your Path to the Kingdom
Diadem Books, 2011
ISBN 978-1-908026-26-2

Hooray! We Have Found the Holy Spirit!
Diadem Books, 2011
ISBN 978-1-908026-354

Hooray! We Have Found the Kingdom!
Diadem Books, 2012
ISBN 978-1-908026-552

HOORAY!

WE HAVE FOUND OUR HERO!

BARBARA FLEMING

MEMOIRS
Cirencester

Published by Memoirs

MEMOIRS
PUBLISHING

25 Market Place, Cirencester, Gloucestershire, GL7 2NX
info@memoirsbooks.co.uk www.memoirspublishing.com

ISBN: 978-1-909304-79-6

And take the helmet of salvation, and the sword of the Spirit,
which is the word of God
(Eph.6:17 KJV)

ACKNOWLEDGEMENTS

Extracts are taken from Gordon of Khartoum: An Extraordinary Soldier by John Pollock published by Christian Focus Publications, Fearn, Ross-shire, Scotland www.christianfocus.com and is used with their permission.

I also want to express my thanks, again, to Jo, of The Bureau, for her great help in preparing the manuscript, and to Joanne and Charles of Diadem Books for again being my all-time angels and producing yet another excellent read for all ages.

TABLE OF CONTENTS

CHAPTER I

WE MEET CHARLES GORDON

Our golden summer had come and gone and now the acorns were falling, like rain, from the spreading oak trees, while the sun was lighting upon a quietly slowing down autumn world.

And here we all were again, sitting together in our comfy chairs, in the fire-light of the flickering flames from our warm, cheerful hearth.

Jane sighted wistfully. "It was such fun finding the Holy Spirit all together, as we did. But I do wish we could have gone on finding it."

There was a thoughtful silence all around the room.

"But," broke in Johnny, "it has helped, hasn't it? And do you know, I asked it to help me in my Science lessons, and it really has. I'm actually beginning to enjoy them!"

"Yes," I agreed. "And it is really helping me to trust in God much, much more completely. And to see all the 'not such nice' things that happen, to be sent for a purpose—or at least to be converted into something good by our lovely Father God."

"But," Barbie announced, from the depths of her chair as usual, "I like my Jesus outside as well, not just tucked away inside. I want to feel His arms all round me when I am sitting all by myself. And I want to hold His hand too when I am walking to school and everywhere."

"Of course, Barbie," I assured her. "He can be both, everything you need. After all, the Bible states clearly 'Underneath are the Everlasting arms.' (Deut.33, 27.)

But out in the busy, noisy World, when we are going so fast from one thing to another, it is such a help to know He is there, within, and protecting and strengthening me all the time."

"I've been thinking about Prayer, though," started up Johnny. "It's about the actual praying.

Most of our prayers seem to consist of *us* doing all the talking—all the asking, especially. If Jesus went off on His own for the whole day—even three or four days as He sometimes did, He wouldn't have been *asking* all the time. He would have been *listening* to His Father, wouldn't He?"

"And thanking Him too," put in Barbie.

"Yes," agreed Jane. "It says He usually went away on His own for one or two hours before the disciples He had been sleeping with had even woken up. I know they sometimes had to go up into the hills to find Him, or watch Him coming back from a distance."

"Mm," pondered Johnny, "Talking of listening to God before you get up in the morning. That sounds sensible, doesn't it? I've always said my prayers at night. But perhaps *starting* the day with them might be a lot more helpful!"

"You may be right there, there, Johnny," I assented. "I have just been reading a book about a man who, all his grown-up life, spent the early two hours, from 6 o'clock to 8 o'clock, every single day, praying, meditating and studying his Bible."

"Goodness!" exclaimed Jane. "Was he a monk or a saint or something?"

"No," I said. "He was a soldier actually. A fighting soldier, all his life, from the age of fifteen when he became a cadet in the Royal Artillery in England. He lived in the middle of the Victorian Age and fought, and commanded, armies all around the world.

Would you like me to tell you about his whole life? He was such a sincere and devoted Christian that I honestly think we ought to have him as our Patron Saint of England instead of this 'St. George (and the Dragon)', nice as he probably was, who never came near our country at all, and someone we hardly know anything about."

"Yes, do tell us about this man. What was his name?" put in Johnny, eagerly.

"He was called Charles Gordon. Only, from his first exciting, and so successful, command in China, he was always known as 'Chinese Gordon'.

He spent his whole life in the army, and was a very friendly and purposeful man, trusting and trustworthy. He was not tall, but his blue eyes shone out strikingly from his ever-alert face.

He started his military life as a Second Lieutenant in

the Royal Engineers and, as your American friend would have surely described him Jane, 'Sure, he was a great guy!' What is more, he is known to have said himself, 'Ever since I can remember, I have believed in Jesus as the Son of God. And I know Him to be my Saviour.'

Although he never married, he always had a wonderful love for children, great and small.

He began to study his Bible, in earnest, in his first army appointment as assistant Garrison Engineer at Pembroke docks in South Wales, and here he 'gave his life to Jesus as his Living Saviour.' Here, too, he read much of Paul's writings, absorbing his 'with me to live is Christ and to die is gain.' From that time on he had no fear of death whatsoever and looked forward to it always with a truly welcoming joy!"

"I guess he spent quite a lot of that 'two hours with God' before he got up in the morning, partly reading his Bible, do you think?" put in Johnny. "Oh dear, it is getting a bit late, isn't it. Please could you tell us everything you know about him tomorrow night?"

"Yes, you are right," I said. "There is *so* much to tell. I think it may take a lot more than one night, too. So goodnight everyone, and sleep well."

CHAPTER II

"A TSUNG PING"

Around the fire we were again, and all agog to hear my story!...

"Gordon," I began, "lived from 1833 to 1885. It was the Victorian Age when England was becoming a great world-imperial power and her armies were scattered the world over.

While, in his first ordering, he was planning and surveying as a Royal Engineer in Pembroke, the Crimean War was being fiercely battled just north of the Black Sea, at Inkerman etc. I am sure you have heard of that awful, and disastrous, 'Charge of the Light Brigade' which had happened then.

But Gordon was just longing to be there, in the thick of it all, as a commander of men!

Finally, in 1855, (when he was 22) he was ordered out as a reserve commander just in time for the last great battle, the siege of Sebastopol, in the sweltering Mediterranean hot summer!

The assaults—and his own gruelling life in the trenches, went on for week after week, Gordon laying mines, as a 'sapper', right under the walls of the town! He had no fear, and was a great leader to all his comrades until, at last, the Russians in the town—firing a last death on 3,000 of the besiegers, withdrew from the town and the fighting was over at last.

But Gordon, among his exhausted compatriots, was as energetic as ever! He had hoped, secretly, to be killed, that he might go to live in that 'other World of his beloved Christ'. Between the actions, in the trenches, amazingly, he was to be found peacefully reading his Bible from cover to cover—while looking forward eagerly to his next assignment from the War Office."

I paused, and Jane turned to Johnny. "You know what I was thinking, Johnny? He was not much older than you are now when he started being a soldier."

"He wasn't a great deal taller, either!" I added, laughing. "For he was always the shortest in his regiment!

But he became a very accurate and skilful surveyor of the new boundaries—needed, for instance, for marking out after peace declarations. But he much preferred to be in the fighting line. So he was very pleased, after a few years of his planning and surveying, to be seconded to China in 1860!

To China, of all places, where some Communist revolutionaries (called the Taipings) were rebelling against the Imperial Chinese Government in Peking. The fighting was mainly in the area near Shanghai and the rebels had taken over many of the scattered town there.

Gordon was now a Major and his job was to prepare for the attacks to be made to re-take all these cities in the desperately ravaged countryside.

He was quite careless of all dangers, always, stealing right up to the foot of the walls to lay mines, study the defences and plan the attacks. His bravery and his leadership of his small regiment, and his tactical skills were literally heroic and produced many brave victories. He became so distinguished for all of it that the Chinese Imperial Government requested that he would become a Major/Colonel in the Imperial Army of China!

Gordon thought very seriously before he would leave the English army and become a Mandarin (taking command of nearly 4,000 men as compared to his tiny English army of 80!)—but he soon became a national hero of China, leading his men to continual victory by the much-improved discipline of his army and his brilliant tactics.

Into the fray he always led them from the front, himself completely unarmed! No sword, no gun, nothing, only waving his cane at the enemy!

He faced the hail of firing with no outward concern and urging his men, with his cane, to a violent fire in return, again and again storming each city until it was taken. And all the time, as he said himself later, 'I used to pray for all my men fighting in the attacks in China, and I would thank God at all times for His hand upon us.' "

"God must have been listening hard to his praying, mustn't He?" announced Jane. "You would think he would have been the first to be killed every time!"

"I would love to have seen him just waving his cane at the enemy though," put in Barbie. "Though I wouldn't have liked all that noise of gunfire and shouting and killing."

"He must have had someone to translate everything from and to the Chinese language, mustn't he?", mused Johnny. "Amazing! Going to a country you hardly know anything about. Not knowing a word of the lingo, and not having a clue what the fighting was all about!"

"And returning, after three years as the greatest commanding hero of the century," I added, "as 'Chinese Gordon'.

Without ceasing, he led his army from battle to battle, storming city after city. He faced terrifying difficulties, treachery and dangers of every kind. He was exposed to personal danger without end in a 'countryside covered in corpses'. But his thorough strategy and skill never deserted him. His planning was skilful in the extreme and he was ever a figure of indomitable will and unceasing energy.

Lastly, in negotiating, he displayed 'an honesty of heart in every word he spoke'.

As one man describes him, 'He was in his late twenties, a light-built, active, wiry, middle-sized man, of dashing qualities as a skilful and dashing commander.' "

"I would love to have really seen him though," said Barbie (from her arm-chair!), "and really met with him."

"Well, that does give us a nice picture of him, doesn't

it?" declared Jane. "Mustn't it have been exciting being in the middle of that huge, totally Chinese, world?"

"Well," I went on, "he became the Chinese equivalent of a brigadier-general (a 'Tsung-ping') and a Mandarin. In fact, to the Chinese he became known as 'Ko-Teng Gordon'. 'Ko' meant 'a charging weapon', and 'Teng' meant 'the arisen one'!

The war against the rebels continued for the years of his magnificent command and was finally won, after 37 successful battles! But it left a countryside, in Southern China, of wasted fields, thousands of massacred bodies, and terrible devastation and misery to the poor people remaining.

All Gordon's' pay was directed to giving them rescue and help. He left China as poor as himself—and as he had entered it—as every penny he had was put to relieving the stress and the starvation of the homeless masses."

"Did the Chinese Government pay him in the end?" asked Jane. "If they thought so highly of him, they must have offered him some money, surely."

"Yes," I said. "They told him they wanted to give him a big box full of silver coins. But Gordon said, 'No, your appreciation and thanks are all I want to take!' So they conferred on him 'the Yellow Jacket', which was the equivalent of our 'Order of the Garter', and was the highest order that can be attained in China.

But when he finally left to come home to England, the stockade where he sailed from was 'ablaze with Chinese lanterns'. Shells and thousands of crackers were let off, and the Imperial army troops, banners, and lanterns blazing, lined his passage for the first mile and a half of his journey!"

"What a lovely send-off," said Barbie. "Even better than our firework night in England!"

"Well, he deserved it," agreed Johnny. "What a way to start your career.

It wasn't a bit like Jesus' life, but it does feel a bit like it somehow,—victorious, loving and being good (and standing up against evil), even if it was in quite a different way.

I can see why you are telling us about him."

"Oh," I laughed, "that is only the beginning of all the things that he did. There is *so* much more! Shall I go on with it tomorrow evening?"

"Yes please," said Johnny. "I can't imagine *what* else he got up to. But I know it would be great to hear it. Let's 'shut up shop' now then, and see you all tomorrow. Goodnight."

CHAPTER III

GORDON'S SECRET

So there we were, all agog to know what had happened next to "Chinese Gordon."

"Now he was a British army Lieutenant-Colonel instead of a Chinese General!" I began.

"After six months leave, he would like to have gone back to China again to renew his work in re-organising their army. But finally it was agreed that he should be given the Senior Officer post of the garrison at Gravesend on the River Thames.

He was thirty-two now (1866)."

"Jesus was not much older than that when he finished his life and died on the cross, was he?" put in Johnny.

"And he had had about as exciting a life, but in a very different way," put in Jane. "Only it ended up with a very different sort of victory than our Chinese Gordon."

"Gordon was a great follower of Jesus in so many ways," I added. "Like Jesus, he never married and had a family, but he loved children—good or bad! In adult life himself, he was a friend you felt you could always trust completely. He was quiet and peaceful within, but full of energy and a joy of living without. Fear was not a word in his vocabulary and, like Paul, he was always convinced that 'to live is Christ, and to die is gain!'

"He still prayed and studied his Bible for at least two hours each morning before 8 o'clock. But he was not wholly convinced that he had found the perfect inner spiritual way of life, even so.

"'I have been thinking wrongly,' he wrote to his mother. 'I have just been praying for the Holy Spirit instead of praying for *more* of it. I know now that that is the answer. And I am sure that the *more* of it will come when I know Christ much more nearly than I do at the moment. He is my friend, but I have looked for Him in all the nineteen chapels and churches in this town—but I found Him in none!'

"So Gordon went on a search for the 'gifts of the Spirit' like we did!" broke in Johnny. "Perhaps *we* should ask for more of them too."

"And he was struggling all on his own," said Jane. "Weren't we lucky to have each other to share our search with?"

"Well, God did answer His prayer very soon," I assured them. "He had been invited to dine, by an army friend of almost royal standing, at Greenwich. Gordon disliked banquets and noisy social occasions at all times, but he accepted the invite from a Crimean War comrade.

In the mansion, in Greenwich, while he was dressing for the dinner, he happened to see a Bible on the table, open at St. John's first gospel. I expect you all know how that letter, brief though it is. It is all about love—the love of God for us and our love for him."

"Yes," chimed in Barbie, "I think it is one of my favourite letters. It is lovely and simple, and direct, and as you say, full of love."

"Well," I continued, "his eye fell on verse 15 in Chapter 4 and he read, 'Whosoever shall confess that Jesus is the Son of God, God dwelleth in him and he in God.' He read it again, and suddenly it was as though he had found a treasure of all time! Yes, of course he believed that Jesus was the Son of God, sent by God, and *now* he must know, for all the rest of his life that God lived right inside him!!

What a wonder. What a buried treasure unearthed! God within him, from now on, every minute of his life! It became 'Gordon's Secret' for all time.

He wrote a 'tract' on it and sent it to all his friends: 'I believe God actually lives in me, in my body and in my soul, and will be living in all others who believe that Jesus Christ is the Son of God. Believe it yourself and ask God to make Himself truly felt by you within—and He will!"

"It was wonderful how it happened, wasn't it?" said Jane. "I think God must work it all out when He wants to get some special truth over to anyone.

You are reading, in your Bible, where you've read many times before and then, suddenly something hits you in a way you never thought of as important before. It has a really deep meaning all of a sudden, meant especially for you."

"Just like when I suddenly realised I hadn't a clue what the Kingdom was," agreed Johnny.

"Yes, that was really wonderful, wasn't it?" I said. "And now this message changed Gordon's whole thinking of God. I think God must have been thrilled too, that His 'Word' to his great worker for Him had been received. To know that God is truly within us is so wonderful, isn't it? And to know that He is there, right inside, guiding every step we take."

I opened my Bible at the Book of Proverbs. "Do listen to what I have found here," I said. "It sums up everything that Gordon found in his 'treasure' that night of the banquet.

> Trust in the Lord, with all your heart,
> And lean not on your own understanding,
> In all your ways acknowledge Him
> And He will direct thy paths.
> *(Prov. 13:3.)*

This is how Gordon lived from then on. With God living within him as a real part of him."

"And directing his path every single day," said Johnny. "Everything that was going to happen to him, from then on, he would be trusting to God as the Steering-wheel of his life."

"And surely, in the same way, *we* should never need to worry about what should happen to us, as God is always in control," added Jane.

"My goodness, that takes an awful lot of worrying out of your life, doesn't it?"

"Yes," I agreed. "No more being anxious as to what will happen… Just complete trust in God to shape it His way—and His way will always be for the good in the end.

I can see why Paul said the fruits of the Spirit were 'love, joy and peace.' It's the peace of not having to worry about things because you can trust *God* in everything."

"And where does Jesus come into this?" mused Johnny.

"Ah yes," I said, "I think I have actually managed to sort that out for myself at last.

Didn't Jesus say 'I am with you always, even until the end of the Earth'? He was with us, besides us, surrounding us with His love—as you said, Barbie. You were absolutely right. Our Father God is within us, our lovely Jesus enfolding us, guiding us, and being always at our side.

I read in one of my books somebody writing, 'He walks with you from room to room.' And how right you are, Jane, to know Him as your best friend!'"

"Oh," put in Barbie, from the depths of her chair, as ever. "Oh, I am so glad He is there, right beside me, with His arms around me, and I can hold His hand from room to room. He is my Jesus."

"And ever be filled with that Christ Spirit that is full of love and power and goodness from our Father God," added Jane. "How right Jesus was when He said you only have to be as simple, and trusting, as a child, to enter his Kingdom. He was talking of ones just like you, Barbie."

"Well, we have learnt and shared a lot tonight, haven't we?" I said. "And we can thank Chinese Gordon for a lot of it. I will tell you all about the rest of his story in Gravesend tomorrow. It is well worth hearing.

Goodnight everyone and sleep well."

CHAPTER IV

THE PATRON SAINT OF GRAVESEND

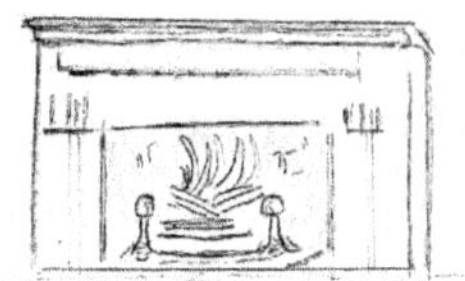

When we were all settled, I started again, "Our Chinese Gordon in Gravesend was living in a large ex-rectory called Fort House, which he felt was really much too big for him. He even had a housekeeper. The house also stood in quite a large, flower-filled garden.

So, being Gordon, he had lots of keys made that fitted the lower garden gate, and passed them around to all the young and old people, who lived near, so they could come and enjoy his garden, sit in it and walk in it, any time they would like.

He loved to see them coming in and enjoying all the flowers and trees and paths. He bought lots of garden seats where they could sit, as long as they liked, to watch the birds flying around in the sunshine. To him it was a real joy. To them it must have seemed like Paradise!"

"Well, it was just about the nearest he could give them to Paradise on Earth, wasn't it?" said Johnny. "A garden of lots of joy!"

"And love," added Barbie. "I don't suppose they knew all that much about God, but somehow a feeling of His love must have got into them, mustn't it?"

"There we go again," said Jane. "He was a sort of modern-day Jesus, wasn't he? Not healing people physically, but perhaps helping to heal their lives."

"Yes," I said, "and after he had finished his paperwork and the walking to examine the restoring of the fortresses along the river that was his job, he would direct his steps down to the dockland side of the river. This was a frontage as dirty and as crowded as any dockland spread!

Up on the hill, behind, were some quite good houses, but towards the docks, on the river-frontage, there was line upon line of miserable terraced hovels. Each 'shack' was backed up by a dark and dirty courtyard with its inevitable shed containing the outside lavatory.

So many were lived in by destitute families, and they were tenements of great poverty and sadness. Gordon was deeply shocked. No, as you said, he was not a healer of sickness as his beloved Christ was, but he determined, himself, to bring healing and joy, in as many ways as possible, to these ragged, joyless folk.

He deliberately turned his steps to the workhouse, and there made contact with a Miss Mary Brown who, he found, ran a 'Soup Kitchen' for this starving part of the city. And, from her, he gathered the names and addresses of the most needful folk.

And then he went back and opened up his house and had some of the worst of the ragged, homeless boys to come and live with him! He bought them new clothes and made it a real home for them.

One or two of them went down with illnesses—scarlet-fever was rife—and these he personally nursed, day and night, until they were well again. Then he would set them to do paid work for him in the garden. Ragged urchins they came in, but became boys finally able to find work in the world outside and quite often on the boats that docked at the harbour on the Thames.

Then Gordon had another idea! He would let even the rest of the children into his garden. There was lots of space, on the lawn, for them to play on. And they wouldn't only play, but be taken into a special corner of the garden where he had a whole stretch of vegetable plots laid out for them to grow food in for their families.

He had to buy the garden tools and seeds for them, but then, his salary was for ever being used to help other people."

"Didn't the children go to school though?" asked Barbie. "That would have kept them off the streets during the day, wouldn't it?"

"No, Barbie," I sadly told her. "There *weren't* any schools for them in those days."

"No schools!" she exclaimed. "Why not?"

"Nobody had thought of setting up the lovely free schools that we were lucky enough to go to; there were paid schools, but the poor people couldn't afford to send their boys there, so they could only play around in the streets all day.

You know 'State Schools' didn't start until nearly the end of the Victorian Era and then it took even longer for girls to be included, instead of only boys."

"Mm," said Barbie thoughtfully. "I am very glad I was born when I was. It takes a lot of thinking about, doesn't it?"

"Yes," I said, "and Gordon was exactly of your thinking too.

There were some small Sunday Schools organised by the chapels and churches in the town. That was a good start. Interestingly, his housekeeper had two sons and even she could not afford to pay to send them to school. So Gordon offered to teach them himself— reading, writing and arithmetic, and quite a lot about our Father God, and Jesus, as well.

It started with the two boys, but soon there were three roomfuls of boys, from the docks and the town, to be taught; by now he had found two helpers from the town churches.

He was a great teacher himself, and genuinely loved the boys however scraggy or badly behaved they were. His teachings were interlaced with lots of references to how lovely Jesus was, and the teaching time always ended with a prayer and a hymn, and then they were all given some money to take home."

"How wonderful that must have been for those boys! To actually learn to read and write in that big (clean) house!" put in Jane. "It must have changed lots of lives!"

"It was a great time for Gordon too. Instead of being saluted and dutifully respected as 'Colonel Gordon', he was 'The Kernel' to his boys, and he called them 'his

Scutters'. One man in the town later wrote of him as 'The finest man in all God's Earth'.

He was so friendly to everybody and good-humoured that he attracted young and old by his kindness. And the way he 'sparkled' somehow, with his clear, blue eyes shining, led another friend in the town to write: 'His eyes seemed to possess a magic power that read you through and through, and loved you as Jesus did!'

If he spotted any boys who looked ill in any way, he would offer to take them home to Fort House and nurse them until they were better. And the very dirty, scraggy ones he would invite in to the house where his housekeeper would patiently scrub them clean and dress them in the new clothes that Gordon was continually buying for them. Then they would be tempted into his 'learning classes' or sent back home with a good, hot drink, food and pocket-money.

As usual, all Gordon's money was spent on helping the poor.

His housekeeper's sons, the start of that 'Schooling', were growing up and, as soon as they had learned enough, Gordon paid for them for a place in a local, private, academy. As he did for many other youngsters.

But he did not only spend his spare time helping the children. He would walk around the town spreading friendship to everyone. He spread his Christian beliefs too, and his continual way of expressing Jesus as his *friend* and ever-helpful and loving companion in such a direct and simple way that spread his faith to all old and young, great and small."

"He did follow Jesus very closely, didn't He, as you

said, Jane?" declared Johnny. "And actually physically healing some of them by nursing. But he did spread a lot of healing in other ways too—being so friendly to everybody, and then doing all that teaching and spending his money for everybody who needed it."

"Yes," I agreed. "I honestly do think he was following that famous declaration of Jesus to the very letter. 'I say to you, as long as you did it to one of these, my least brethren, you did it unto me.' (Matt. 23:40.)

Doesn't it lift you up, somehow, to think about it? I think that is what real saints are made of.

Not that Gordon would have liked you to tell him how wonderful he was. He never liked praise, or thanking at all.

But he was the greatest man who ever lived in Gravesend. And he is not forgotten there by a statue of himself, still standing and unhurt through two World Wars, in the 'Gordons' Memorial Garden'—the patron saint of Gravesend, Chinese Gordon!

I'll stop there for now. There is so much more to tell. So goodnight everyone and God bless!"

This is what is written at the base of the statue:-

General Charles C. Gordon C.B.

This statue is dedicated to the memory of
General Gordon who so faithfully served
the poor of this borough between the years 1865 to 1871.

Together with his modernisation of New Tavern Fort
and other forts along the Thames. He is best remembered
for his generosity and his struggle to give the benefits
of education to the poor of this town.
General Gordon was murdered during the Siege of Khartoum
and departed this life
26th January 1885.
R.I.P.

CHAPTER V

GORDON FIGHTS THE SLAVE TRADE

Settled again for the evening, I continued straight away to tell the story of our Chinese Gordon. All were agog to hear it.

I began: "Now we know that Jesus had such a lot of opposition from the Pharisees, and other Elders of the Temple, in his wonderful work. And, in the same way Gordon came up against jealousy, deceit and other hostilities in his military and diplomatic life after that 'homely' post in Gravesend.

He was seconded to this country and that, but not often to lead in any warlike campaigns although he was still a soldier.

Firstly he was sent to Romania as 'Commissioner' on the Danube River. Then back to Sebastopol to Turkey and report on the military cemeteries there. After this he was ordered out to Egypt, to become 'Gordon Pasha', under the Khedive Ismail, ruler, to attempt to put an end to the infamous slave trade in Egypt and the neighbouring country of Sudan."

"There were slaves right back in Jesus' time, weren't there?" put in Johnny. "I remember reading about one that Paul looked after."

"And the Romans made slaves of English people when they came here, too," said Jane.

"And we bought them to work on the plantations in America too, didn't we?" added Johnny. "But we knew it was wrong and had stopped it."

"You are all right," I said, "but, sadly, the slave-trade in Africa, at that time, was horrific! It was being practised all over the Continent by hundreds of traders who seized young and old victims from the helpless native tribes, greedily selling them, mainly from the East Coast, for money. In fact it had become the chief source of income in the commerce of much of tribal Africa.

It was heartlessly cruel and pitiless and savage and most of the European World was now keen to see it eradicated. (Though the Portuguese were still much involved in lands south of the Equator.)

So Gordon landed in Egypt and, using the River Nile mostly for Transport, sailed into the Sudan with a small team of supporters. He was now His Excellency 'Gordon Pasha, Governor General of the Equator', because the Sudan stretches south almost to the Equator, nearly 700 miles from the city he had centred himself, in Khartoum.

Up and down the Nile he sailed to challenge the slave-traders. He caught slaves and released them and soon came to be heralded as the 'God' of the native peoples. He was impatient to cleanse the whole region. As usual his tactics were impeccable in cleansing the southern area of the hideous slave-trade. He rarely used force but worked hard re-organising the local tribes to peace and stopped the slave-trade with a confident determination which overcame all dangers and difficulties.

Yes, he would disappear for times of reading his Bible and praying. He wrote constant letters to his friends and family. When force *was* needed he, of course, led his little band, waving his stick at his opponents. But most of the good work seems to have been by gentle, persuasive and agreeable speaking.

Eventually he returned, triumphant, to Khartoum, where he was also glad to help the various missionary workers there. For the 'Christianising' of the Sudan was his deepest aim.

'How he loved the native people,' wrote one of his companions. He was still the eager, friendly, follower of his God. Later the same man wrote, 'Your kindness will *never* be forgotten here!'

But the years went by and, over such a huge area, trying to bring it all to goodness and safety became a very hard and draining task. Gordon found it exhausting in the end and referred to it as his 'crucifixion'!"

"There, another comparison with Jesus," exclaimed Johnny. "What a brave, wonderful chap he was!"

"He must have felt awful to have to say that though, mustn't he?" added Jane. "Did he ever see the end of it?"

"Well, he was there for a gruelling five years altogether," I told them. "He accomplished what he had been sent out for although he had to put up with much diplomatic double-dealing, from both Egypt and England. His final ordeal was to go into Abyssinia and meet its King (John) to conclude negotiations there. This he had to do after over a month of very difficult travelling through rugged, mountainous country.

King John was a so-called Christian but actually was just about the cruellest man you could ever imagine. He loved cutting off people's ears, noses and hands. But mostly he revelled in putting out their eyes!

He had his head-clerk beaten by fifty lashes in Gordon's presence! For Gordon it was surely not far off the experience of our St. George meeting with the Dragon."

"Goodness!" exclaimed Johnny. "Even the Pharisees weren't as cruel as that, were they?"

"Well, they were to animals," put in Jane. "Wasn't it good when Jesus set them all free that time in the Temple? And, do you know, Barbie and I were reading about her beloved David, in the book of Kings the other day, and we came to where his son, Solomon, was celebrating building the first temple in Jerusalem, and it says: 'And Solomon offered a sacrifice to the Lord of two and twenty thousand oxen and a hundred and twenty thousand sheep!' (I Kings 8: 63)."

"That sounds horrific," I said. "How God must have hated it.

And Gordon, as you can imagine, did not get on at all well with this King John who said straight to him, 'You know, Gordon Pasha, I could kill you, on the spot, if I liked!'

But Gordon answered him, 'Go ahead and kill me then. I should love to die. In fact you would be doing me a favour and saving me from all the troubles that may still be in store for me!'

So the 'Dragon' was 'vanquished' there and Gordon returned safe and sound to Khartoum, and eventually to Cairo and to England."

"I think that was lovely," said Jane, "and he really meant what he said so bravely. It is just like St. Paul writing as you said, 'for me to live is Christ and to die is gain,' isn't it?" (Phil. 1:21.)

"Yes," I said, "and you really feel, don't you, that what our Chinese Gordon says, he actually does believe with all his heart. But now, after five years of his great work in the Sudan—and with all his wise suggestions, as to how the governing there should be continued, completely discarded by those in charge in England and Egypt, he retired to a much-needed freedom and rest." There was a sigh of relief from the armchairs, so I went on, "Not having a family home left in England now, Gordon decided to spend his leave in Switzerland and enjoy a few months of peace in the peace and beauty of that lovely country."

"Switzerland never fights in wars, does it?" put in Jane. "How sensible of it, and it must be a really good place to rest in."

"And Gordon, as friendly as ever, made many good friends there. One of them wrote of him later: 'There was a lovely charm about him. I shall always remember his kindliness and the way he brightens up every room he walks into. And what struck me most was his oneness with God, and the way he shared all his daily life with him.'

Most of all he loved being with the children, playing with them and always telling them about Jesus. It was a really happy time and Gordon returned refreshed and, as usual, ready for any call (from his God!) to duty."

"It must have been pretty hard not knowing where on Earth you were going to be sent next," said Johnny. "He didn't seem to mind it all, did he? Just left it to God always to choose the right way and to see him safely through it. I call that being strong and brave. A real St. George to fight every dragon."

"He certainly was such a strong man, wasn't he?" I said. "And such a kindly one, too, to everybody.

He spent a very short while in India and also a brief time in his beloved China. China, at that time, seemed to be on the brink of war with Russia, but were fortunately drawn off it by Gordon's wise intervention.

After this he was sent to Mauritius and then Cape Town. He met with Rhodes in Basutoland and visited an Anglican Mission where the Reverend John Widdcombe later wrote of him: 'I never met a man so saturated in scriptural knowledge—especially the Old Testament. He struck me as a really humble-minded Christian who was penetrated with the mind and spirit of Christ… He was a devout soldier of God.' "

"Oh," said Barbie. "I do like that, 'a soldier of God.' That describes him perfectly, doesn't it? So like my beloved King David, ready to fight for any evil, but always spreading peace and real fellowship for his Lord."

"That sums him up beautifully, Barbie," I answered. "Shall we close down now, on that lovely thought, for the night? There is yet more coming tomorrow.

Goodnight, everyone, and sleep well."

CHAPTER VI
THE HOLY LAND

Our little group was comfortably, as usual, waiting eagerly for another chapter in the ways and life of our Chinese Gordon.

"I wonder where he is off to today," ventured Johnny.

"Goodness knows," said Jane. "What a life he had, travelling, travelling, travelling."

"But always with his lovely Bible in his luggage," put in Barbie. "He must have known most of it by heart by now."

"Well," I said, "for once he chose his own, long journey. Now he planned to go to the very heart of his Jesus' world—the land of the Bible! And he set off, eastwards, to spend nearly a whole year in the actual home of his beloved Jesus, the Holy Land of Israel!"

"Oh," said Jane, "how wonderful! I should love to go there and see all the places where Jesus actually walked, where he healed people and told everybody His wonderful news about God being their Father. Where

He was born in that stable in Bethlehem and where He lived with His fishermen in Capernaum."

"Yes," I agreed. "The most miraculous and glorious place on Earth. Though sadly ruined at that time as it was ruled by a non-Christian Arab government from Turkey, as part of Syria.

Fortunately, during the First Great War, British troops were sent out to that part of the world—you have heard of some of the victories of Lawrence of Arabia.

And by the end of the war the Turks had been driven out and Israel was entrusted to the Mandate of Britain, governed by a High Commissioner.

When I was out in the Holy Land, thirty years ago, I was talking to an Arab in Jerusalem one day and what he said was so uplifting. He said, "Do you know, the years we were under British rule was the only time, in our whole history that we have experienced good and fair government!"

"That makes you really proud of being British, doesn't it," announced Johnny. "And wasn't it nice of the Arab to say it?"

"Yes," I said. "Gordon would have been glad to hear it too, for when he arrived there the buildings in Jerusalem were decayed, there were Mohammeddan spires and domes everywhere, and the remains of the Jewish Temple was now 'The Wailing Wall' to the Jews who had started filtering back to their 'homeland' mainly from Russia after the Crimean war.

But Gordon, friendly as ever, made himself known to them as a 'common or garden' traveller, and as usual, emptied his pockets of all his money to help them in their poverty.

But, remember that he was a Royal Engineer by service, and that meant that he was (among other things) a surveyor.

He was very excited when he visited the site called Golgotha where his beloved Christ, his friend and saviour, had been crucified.

Examining it with the greatest care and measuring it up with all the descriptions of it in our Bible, he came to the conclusion that the accepted present site was not correct.

Being Gordon, he mapped out an alternative area which seemed more accurate to him and then he went on to position the small cave in a wonderful little garden surrounding it which he felt was the original tomb for Christ's body.

What is so nice to know now is that this Garden (and the cave within it) was bought by England and is still English Property, run by English people. And it can be visited and deeply enjoyed by us at all times."

"I think I am going to go there when I grow up," stated Jane firmly. "A garden for Jesus, what could be lovelier?"

"Yes," I said. "I hope you will all go and see it one day. To me it was 'the heart of the Holy Land'."

"But Gordon visited all the other well-known sites of Jesus' life, didn't he?" enquired Johnny.

"Well, He had a whole year to travel around. He went to Capernaum with its still-standing ruins of its Third Century synagogue. That would have been full of memories of Jesus teaching and healing. And then he rented a 'cottage' at Ain Karem, where John the Baptist had lived, to be central for all the country.

Every minute of his year in Israel was filled with wonderful thoughts of thankfulness for the life of his Jesus."

"Did he visit Bethlehem too? I should love to see the stable where Jesus was born and all the donkeys and everything," put in Barbie.

"Yes, Barbie," I assured her. "There is a big church there now, over where they think the stable was. And the placing of his manger is right down in the heart of it, marked with a golden star.

Did you know that St. Francis of Assisi visited the Holy Land, right in the middle of the Crusaders fighting there? And when he came back he made that first stable scene for some villagers in Italy, all complete with a donkey and an ox? You can still meet lovely Franciscans looking after some of the Holy sites. I am sure Gordon must have met with them too.

He wrote many letters to his friends in England to tell them all about it—how he rode his mule or donkey, or rode in a rough carriage from place to place, from Jericho to Haifa, from Jaffa to Jerusalem.

One missionary man he was staying with in Gaza called on his door while his morning two-hour studying and praying was in progress. And he happened to see the list of the people he was praying for. It numbered nearly three hundred!

"Goodness, that *is* a lot!" exclaimed Johnny. "I don't

think I would even *know* that number of people, let alone pray for them!"

"Well, perhaps we had better be off to bed to say our prayers (and read our Bibles like Gordon) either tonight or tomorrow morning," I said. "And tomorrow we shall see what followed Gordon's wonderful year in Israel when he returned to 'all the perils' of the Wide world.

Goodnight everyone, and God bless."

CHAPTER VII

THE SUDAN

We were round our hearth again and all excited to hear more about our Chinese Gordon.

"Oh," I began, "I forgot to mention that the story of St. George and his dragon actually began during the Crusader wars in the Holy Land.

Apparently George had been killed by heretics for his faith in Christ and earned his sainthood that way. And then, for some reason or another, the Crusaders brought the story of him back to England."

"So he never lived in England, did he?" stated Johnny firmly. "I wonder where the 'dragon' bit came in."

"Well," I laughed, "the nearest you can get to dragons, out East, would be a crocodile from the River Nile!

Ah well, the rest of Chinese Gordon's story comes from the Nile area of Egypt and the Sudan, but no crocodiles are included. The dragon Gordon had to face there was a bloodthirsty Arab known as 'The Mahdi'.

It started off in Jaffa when Gordon had been eight months in the Holy Land. There he received a telegram telling him that the King of Belgium—King Leopold—was asking for Gordon to oversee the re-organising of the Belgian Congo for him. Telegrams went backwards and forwards from Belgium and London and, a month later, Gordon left the Holy Land and journeyed to Brussels to work out his going to the Congo for his Majesty, King Leopold.

Unfortunately, at the same time, this Mahdi-led 'revolution' was growing more and more threatening in the Sudan, and Gordon's name was put forward as the only person who could sort things out there."

"So he didn't get to the Belgium Congo then?" put in Johnny. "I don't think I should have been too keen to go there—all wet and hot and thickly forested."

"But what a life he led, didn't he?" said Jane. "Sent this way and that, all over the world, and mostly into danger."

"That was one of the things that was so wonderful about him," I put in. "He always said, 'Whatever God wants me to do, wherever he directs me, that is always the right place for me to go, however horrible it looks!' What a trust he had, didn't he? 'Fear not' I think must have been his watchword."

"Yes," said Jane. "Definitely our Patron saint too. It would have been wonderful to have actually met him and to have heard him always talking of Jesus being his all-time friend. Wasn't he lovely?"

"Yes," I went on. "But I think he was quite keen to go back and meet all the people in the Sudan again and help them. A friend of his tells us in one of his letters, 'He loved the ordinary people of the Sudan so much!'"

"But why should the conditions in the Sudan be of such interest to us in England?" asked Johnny. "It wasn't a part of our Victorian empire, was it? And Egypt, next-door to it, where Gordon had started from at first, was nothing really to do with us either."

"I think," I said, "it was probably basically that the Suez Canal had been carved through from the Mediterranean to the Red Sea only recently, and that had made an enormous difference to our journeying, and contact with, Southern India, Australia, New Zealand, and the Far East. And our Prime Minister of that time (Disraeli) had bought a large amount of the shares in it. And it was right next-door to Egypt! So we wanted a nice peaceful Egypt and not one that seemed to be at continual loggerheads with the Sudan which was next door to it.

Egypt thought it ought to rule the Sudan but was a very bad ruler indeed. So, what with renewed slave-trading and very bad interference into it, from Egypt, Sudan had become a part of our interest again."

"Is it a very big country then?" asked Jane. "I don't think I know much about it."

"Well, it stretches well over a thousand miles from the southern edge of Egypt practically to the Equator, to the boundary of what was Uganda. A lot of the northern part is desert, but the southern half is tropical grassland.

The River Nile runs right through it, from the South, near the Equator, to the Mediterranean Sea in the North (through Egypt). And part of the eastern coast of it runs down the western side of the Red Sea, below the Suez Canal.

The Chief town in it is Khartoum which is a big walled city where Gordon had centred himself when he was there before. Khartoum is on the River Nile which winds in a large loop when it reaches the northern demi-desert area, of the Sudan from Egypt, but eventually reaches Khartoum well over a thousand miles (2,000 kilometres) from Cairo in Egypt."

"Thank you," said Johnny. "I'm beginning to get a better idea of the layout of things now. It was an enormous country, wasn't it? But not unified in any way, just local tribes and half desert. Very vulnerable to a greedy country next door, as Egypt sounds to be. Were they Christians in any way?"

"There were missionaries for Christianity at some places in it," I answered. "Mohammedism had spread in from Egypt and all the northern part of Africa."

"Well, we are talking about life in a very, very different country altogether, from what we are used to in England. I can just see them on their camels and donkeys," put in Jane. "And on their little boats up and down the river."

"I think I am learning a bit of geography as well as the life and times of Chinese Gordon." Johnny smiled. "But it is getting rather late. Do let us hear all about his next adventure tomorrow night. I'm off to bed now. Goodnight everyone, Goodnight!"

CHAPTER VIII

A JOURNEY DOWN
THE RIVER NILE

Here we were again, all gathered to hear what was to be the final chapter in the story of our lovely Chinese Gordon.

I started off: "As they say, all good things do come to an end, and the end of this story is very exciting!

First of all, while Gordon was out in the Holy Land, there had been a rebellion in Egypt against the government of the Khedive. In the riots in Alexandria at least fifty Europeans had been killed, so a British army had been sent out to quell the revolutionaries and an English diplomat appointed to take over the ruling. Thankfully, that did bring peace there for the next thirty years.

But Egypt still had small garrisons scattered round the north of the Sudan—dating from when it was trying to set a foothold in the governing of that country.

Perhaps the uprising in Egypt encouraged the

Sudanese to rise up against these garrisons, for suddenly a very dangerous rebellion had broken out in the Sudan led by a Moslem fanatic called the Mahdi. Ostensibly it was a rising against Egyptian 'rule'."

"Not *another* revolution," broke in Johnny. "Another killing?"

"Yes," I said sadly. "What a lot of killing has been a part of the history of our world. It is sad, isn't it?"

"Our Bible says: 'Love your neighbour as yourself'," put in Jane. "If we all did *love* our neighbours, perhaps there wouldn't be any more wars.

Jesus always did it in the peaceful, loving way, didn't He?"

"But isn't it good that we only actually remember the names of the ones who were killed, like all the martyrs, and not the names of the people who killed them?" said Barbie slowly, from the depths of her arm-chair.

"Now there's simple philosophy for you," returned Johnny. "Yes, let's look on the bright side of wars and everything. To die means you are leaving this Earth and going to somewhere much, much, lovelier, like Chinese Gordon always said. He told that Abyssinian King that he would be doing him a favour, didn't he?"

"Yes, and he never grieved at all when his near-by family died. What a wonderful faith he had! And how wonderfully it held him through this last year of his life," I went on.

"Things were getting worse and worse in the Sudan. Lots more killing by the Mahdi and his followers. Finally the people in England decided they *must* do something about it. Egyptians must be completely cleared out of the Sudan and peace must be established there to protect all the defenceless native tribes.

And now, of course, after his very successful (but only temporary apparently) settling of the Sudan before, Chinese Gordon was the obvious choice to send out to bring stability and peace in the country.

Gordon was quite keen himself. As I said, he had really loved the simple, native folks there. So a telegram was sent to King Leopold, with many apologies, asking him to keep the Congo Governorship 'on hold' for a few months until Gordon had settled the Sudan."

"They did seem to do a lot of informing by telegram in those days, didn't they?" said Johnny. "Did they write many letters?"

"Oh yes," I answered him. "Gordon was a great writer. He wrote letters and tracts by the dozen. He was always putting his thoughts down on paper and sending them to all his friends and associates."

"I guess that is why we know as much about him now," agreed Johnny. "How sensible."

"He wrote to all his friends, and especially to his sister, to tell them of his next assignment and to ask for their special prayers for his success there. To one friend he wrote that he felt such an upliftment when he prayed for him at his prayer meeting. 'And now,' he wrote, 'I shall calmly rest on the will of God, whose will it is, I am sure, that I am being sent to do His work.'

Then, of course, he had to check that all the pensions he paid (out of his salary), to many old folk, would be safely continued in his absence. And the monies he had assigned to many young boys to continue their schooling.

When he arrived at the station in London, to begin his journey to Egypt and the Sudan, the Lords and Generals etc., seeing him off, had to buy his rail ticket for him and provide him with a pocket full of money, as he had none of his own!

It was the middle of winter (January 14th 1884) when he set out, as Major General Charles Gordon, as he was now, and he arrived by steamer in Egypt ten days later."

"At least he would have been sailing into a nice Mediterranean winter, much warmer than in England, wouldn't he?" answered Johnny.

"How many soldiers did he have with him in his army, this time?" asked Jane?

"No, he wasn't given any military support at all this time," I said. "It was supposed to be just a clearing out of the families of the Egyptians who had lived in the little garrisons in the northern desert of the Sudan. And then a peaceful settlement was expected, with the Mahdi, so that now the Sudan could settle down to a quiet, unhostile, native government."

"That sounds nice and easy," put in Johnny, "but he would have a long sail down the River Nile to get into the Sudan to start with, wouldn't he?" He stated firmly, "Boats wouldn't be going very fast in those days, I am sure."

"He had arrived at Port Said on the 24th of January," I told him. "Then he travelled down to call in at Cairo, and then it was eight days steaming to the Sudan Border. He had one or two companions to support him and, at the border, they had to transfer to camels to ride through the desert for six days across the loop the river makes there, and the cataracts on it. And then it was back onto the Nile again and they reached Khartoum sometime in February."

"What a journey!" added Jane. "But at least it wouldn't have been too hot, even across the desert."

"But every place they touched at, on the journey, the people there had greeted him with almost overwhelming joy, which was really lovely. 'Our "master" has come back to us,' they cried!

And when he eventually arrived at Khartoum the welcome he got there was almost unbelievable! They kissed his hands, they kissed his feet! And then, through a guard of honour, dressed in magnificent uniforms, he was escorted to the palace and led to ascend a special 'pulpit' which they had raised where he could address the crowd. His voice rang out over the mass of heads, assuring them that his Almighty God would be their strength and their protector from now on!

Actually I thought how like, it was, to that triumphal ride of Jesus down the Mount of Olives on the donkey. Didn't the crowds that lined His route there shout, 'Hooray! Our Saviour King has come,' and spread their clothes on His way in triumph and adoration!"

"Why yes," broke in Jane. "Just like Jesus again. How wonderful!"

"I do wish I had been that donkey," added Barbie. "He must have felt so proud, actually carrying Jesus, mustn't he?"

"That's a great thought, Barbie," agreed Johnny. "Perhaps we could all think of ourselves as the simple 'donkey carriers' of Jesus!"

"Yes," I said, "that is truly a wonderful thought. And Gordon had surely come to his Jerusalem, as Jesus had. Shall I stop there, on that lovely note, for tonight and I will end our story tomorrow?

Goodnight everyone, and sleep well."

CHAPTER IX

EATEN BY THE DRAGON

There was a strange feeling in the air as we settled ourselves around our fireside this evening. What was going to happen to Gordon to make this our last chapter?

"He had been sent out with only two missions to accomplish," *I* began. "Firstly, to see that the soldiers and their families in the small Egyptian garrisons were sent back, safely, up the Nile to Egypt. Then he was to communicate with the Mahdi and, since the purpose of his uprising will have been reached, invite him to be part of a peaceful administration for the Sudan.

So Gordon had already written to the Mahdi to open the negotiations, while he was on the last stretch of his journey, to offer him a large sum of money to help with the evacuation of the garrisons and his own settlement, and to offer him part governorship of the Country.

But the answer he received when he had become settled in Khartoum was horrific!

The Mahdi was obviously not the sincere, and

genuine fighter just for the freedom, and good, of the Sudan as he had claimed to be. He was an Arab Muslim whose one aim was to kill all non-Muslims and to make himself the blood-thirsty dictator of the whole Country.

He demanded Gordon's immediate surrender of Khartoum, and become a Muslim himself or he would be killed like every other Sudanese who refused to accept his religion!!"

"Poor Gordon!" exclaimed Jane. "How terrible for him. He was such a wonderful believing Christian too!"

"I think we are back to 'the Dragon' again," declared Johnny. "St George and his dragon, and now Chinese Gordon and his Mahdi! And the fight sounds as though it was going to be just as bloodthirsty!"

"Yes," I said, "a replica of St George's dragon the Mahdi certainly was, with a still ever-growing army at his back. And it was more than clear to Gordon that Khartoum was going to be besieged unless he could find a large enough army to repulse him. And even from the town itself, frightened Sudanese were going over to the Mahdi camp, and the raising of a big enough army to overthrow the Mahdi forces was becoming daily more impossible.

Telegrams and letters went backwards and forwards to Cairo and to England: "Peace can only be gained here now by armed force! We are besieged! I need British troops to save ourselves here and the whole Sudan!"

"There go the telegrams again," said Johnny. "What a good thing they had been invented."

"But, of course, Gordon was not one to just sit back and wait for help. Being a Royal Engineer of high skills he saw that fortification posts were established and guarded all around the city. He laid mines outside the walls and also saw to the river-side defences against the enemy forces on the opposite bank of the Nile.

In England, sadly, the present head of Government, the Prime Minister, a man called Gladstone, had no interest whatsoever in what happened overseas. He ignored the pleas of all the Country to send help to Gordon!

"How could he be so awful?" put in Jane. "He sounds a very bad Prime Minister."

"Even the Queen (Victoria) wrote to him to rescue Gordon," I added. "And, by the way, the Mahdi had then cut off the way of the Nile, so no more letters could get through.

But Gordon stood his ground! He still gave the first two hours of each day to his Bible-reading, praying and sharing his thoughts with God. He liked best to sit right up on the flat roof of the Palace completely regardless of the continual sniping at him from across the river. His helpers pleaded with him not to use any lights up there, to help the enemy. But being Gordon he doubled the lighting…

He had bands playing at weekends to cheer the townspeople and, because there was constant shooting from beyond the walls and much injury to the guards, he saw that the hospital was run well and the men nursed and cheered-up. Food was running short so he carefully apportioned it all. The weeks went by… the telegrams kept going… High Summer came—and at last Gladstone was persuaded to send an army to help!"

"Oh, how wonderful!" cried Barbie. "God working right at last! But wasn't Gordon ever so brave to stay and get Khartoum all fortified like that. After all, he *could* have sailed back to safety as soon as he had received the Mahdi's letter, couldn't he?"

"Yes," I agreed. "In fact, the man who finally led the relief column, Sir Garnet Wolesley, later wrote to a relative of Gordon, that 'Your Gordon is the only man I have ever known who can claim to be a "Real Hero!"'".

Wolesley landed in Egypt in September and he made straight for Cairo and assembled a force of ten thousand men. But the journey ahead of them was going to be a thirteen hundred mile march and sail to bring relief to Khartoum. It would take months!"

"Oh, if only they had had aeroplanes in those days," said Jane. "Aeroplanes would have done it in days!"

"Yes, but both sides would have had them, remember," put in Johnny. "And Khartoum would probably have been a bombed-out wreck, like our Coventry in the last war."

"Well," I said, "in the meantime Gordon did his best to keep up everybody's spirits. He rode a horse round the defences every day in spite of the continuous gunfire and explosions. His native soldiers all loved him.

In the night he could be found (up on the roof) writing down all the happenings of the day, *and* all his thoughts on the subject *and* continually to trust in God to bring His good out of all evil."

"What a wonderful trust he had in God, didn't he? And it was good of him to go on writing all his letters and reports to his family and friends etc., although he knew he could never post them now," said Jane.

"And think of him doing it all—plus his Bible-reading, praying and meditation—right on the roof of his palace within such easy reach of the continuous shooting across the river," I added. "And often must he have gone up there too, in the daytime and looked expectantly up the length of the river to see if any help was coming!

Week after week went by and, by the end of October, the Mahdi's huge force had closed in tightly around Khartoum. They were hoping, at last, to starve the city into final submission."

"Oh, if only the relieving force could have gone faster!" cried Barbie. "If only they would come!"

"You share Gordon's thoughts absolutely, Barbie," I answered. "December came and went and the starving city, and Gordon, still hung on. He kept telling everybody that help was nearly here—then he would be up on the roof again writing down his thoughts in his journal and assuring himself that his God, and his Jesus, were to be trusted in victory, and even death in defeat!

On January 26th there was a betrayal by a small group of the terrified townsfolk in a corner of the wall and at last the Mahdi broke through into the city, and, it is said, that 40,000 men of the Mahdi's army charged into the streets killing all who would not join them!

Gordon, from his rooftop, stepped down and, at the top of the stairs that led down to the street below, faced the bloodthirsty horde, completely fearless and unarmed.

He looked steadily at them, threw open his tunic and

shouted, "Kill me as you will!" The spear was flung into his heart and he dropped dead upon the steps!

But at last he could rise into that wonderful other-life that he so longed to live in, that Kingdom of his wonderful God and his beloved Son, Jesus Christ! And how truly he could say, with Paul, 'I am ready! I have fought a good fight, I have kept the faith. I have finished the course prepared for me by God my Father.'

And like Jesus, perhaps he also said within: 'Into thy hands I commend my spirit…'

Two days later the rescuing army arrived!

"Poor Gordon. Although I know he would have been ever so glad to die," said Barbie thoughtfully. "Just like St. George being eaten by the dragon. And he really was a martyr, wasn't he?"

"Yes," I said. "He was wonderful staying on in Khartoum when he could have easily returned to safety in the beginning. I think he must have known, all along, that he might have to die for his much loved people of the Sudan."

"What happened to all of them?" asked Johnny. "Were they all killed too?"

"No," I said. "Many of them did manage to survive. And you will be pleased to know that, under another Prime Minster, an army-commander called Lord Kitchener was sent out with an English/Egyptian army to bring peace to the Sudan at last in 1898. After that it was known as the 'Anglo-Egyptian Sudan'."

"But he did have to face that 'Mahdi-dragon', just like our Sr. George is supposed to have done," claimed Jane. "And be killed by it too."

"And he did it as an Englishman," put in Barbie.

"Yes," said Johnny. "I think I am going to make him *my* 'up to date' Patron Saint. He was a Super Christian. His ever-trust in God, and his love for Jesus Christ were just terrific. You are right to say he deserves to be called a Saint—a really truly brave one too.

He is going to be my Patron Saint of England, for always."

"And mine too," agreed Jane.

"And mine too," broke in Barbie. "He didn't ride on a donkey, but he did ride on a camel you said, and he helped so many people who needed help as Jesus did. And he was always telling them about how wonderful his God was, too.

And that awful last year in Khartoum was almost like being hung up on a cross, in a way, wasn't it? Only it went on lots and lots longer.

If anybody could have lived as beautifully as Jesus lived, I think it was your Great Chinese Gordon.

It was so lovely hearing all about his life—and even his death (although that *was* sad!). He is going to be my special hero from now on."

"Well," I said, "now you have heard the story of Chinese Gordon. A story to be so proud of, and so uplifting, I am so glad you enjoyed it.

Despite all the wars in our history, and the killings,

there have been so many wonderful people in our history that we can be proud of. And so many truly believed in God as our Great Father and His loving ever-beside-us Son, Christ Jesus, and lived as real Saints.

The last thing the humble Chinese Gordon would have wanted, of course, was to be proclaimed as a Saint. But he stands high in our history as one of our greatest heroes and a truly brilliant and magnificent Christian in the truest sense of the words for all time.

I hope you will all sleep well after such an exciting story. And I know you will say, with me, 'Thank you wonderful Chinese Gordon, you are our hero and can be our Patron Saint.'

Good night and God bless you all."

www.ingramcontent.com/pod-product-compliance
Lightning Source LLC
Chambersburg PA
CBHW061053050726
47592CB00004B/1652